AF469632

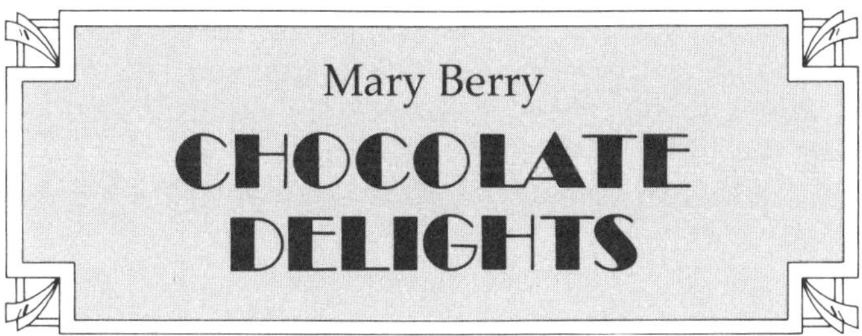
Mary Berry
CHOCOLATE
DELIGHTS

Mary Berry

CHOCOLATE DELIGHTS

PIATKUS

First published in 1985 by
Judy Piatkus (Publishers) Ltd, London

British Library Cataloguing in Publication Data
Berry, Mary, *1935–*
Chocolate Delights.
1. Cookery (Chocolate)
I. Title
641.6'374 TX767.C5
ISBN 0–86188–370–5

Edited by Susan Fleming
Designed and illustrated by Paul Saunders

Typeset by Phoenix Photosetting, Chatham
Printed and bound by Mackays of Chatham Ltd, Kent

CONTENTS

Acknowledgements

When I began working on *Chocolate Delights* it seemed a somewhat daunting project, but it quickly became evident that the problem was not what to include, rather what to leave out!

Three of us worked on the book and I want to thank my two assistants – Debbie Woolhead and Anne Byerley. Debbie, who is such a pleasure to work with, is meticulous and professional – and a great expert in cake-making and icing. Anne, a home economics student from Sheffield Polytechnic, helped us with the recipe testing. Her special favourite, which was tested two or three times until we got it absolutely perfect, was Peanut Butter Crunch. My special thanks to both of them.

INTRODUCTION

Chocolate is everybody's favourite flavour. Brightly wrapped bars piled up on sweet shop counters, or grouped temptingly round the supermarket checkout; rich, smooth confections in elaborate boxes that are works of art in themselves, tributes for Mother's Day or to a beloved; the quick snack that restores flagging energy, pampers a sweet tooth and swallows up children's pocket money. . . Chocolate is as you want it. And how we all love it! We appreciate it, too, for its generous gifts to cookery – the rich chocolate cake, the icing, the soufflé, the pudding, the ice cream. The taste is adored by everyone.

The History of Chocolate

It is a bit of a shock to realise that chocolate in its familiar eating form has existed for not much more than a hundred years. Fry's Chocolate Cream Bar was launched in 1866 and is still a best-seller; Cadbury's Dairy Milk dates from 1905; and it was not until the year of 1932 that the Mars Bar was born.

These are the results of modern technology and expertise, but chocolate itself, the product of the cocoa bean, has been enjoyed by man for at least 3,000 years. Its known history begins with the Aztecs and Mayans of Central America, where the cacao or cocoa tree flourishes. They used the beans to make a bitter, spiced drink which they valued so highly that even the planting of the tree had a special ritual of its own, while the drink had important ceremonial functions. The beans were used as currency, and were also an ingredient of savoury dishes, used in a spiced sauce served with game. Even today, turkey or chicken in chilli and chocolate sauce is Mexico's special dish, served on festive occasions.

The first cocoa beans were brought to Europe in 1502 by Christopher Columbus, but the beans do not at first seem to have

made much of an impression on the Spaniards. A few years later, however, Cortes and his conquistadors were hospitably entertained to the drink called *xocoatl* (literally 'bitter water') at the court of the Emperor Montezuma, where it was served highly spiced and stirred to a froth. Cortes recognised its energy-giving properties and on his return home he introduced the strange drink to the Spanish court. Too bitter for European tastes, it was made acceptable by the addition of sugar and vanilla, themselves recent introductions from the New World, and it quickly became fashionable at the Spanish court.

Spain jealously guarded its secret for almost a hundred years. During this time cocoa became the subject of religious controversy and there was much learned argument as to whether it was a drink or a food and whether it might be permitted on fast days. An Italian visitor to Spain in 1606 took the recipe for the chocolate drink home with him and a century later the coffee houses of Venice and Florence had become famous for their chocolate.

It had reached France by the late sixteenth century (brought by the Jews driven out of Spain), but it was not until the marriage about a hundred years later of Louis XIV to the Spanish princess Maria Theresa, who had an insatiable passion for it, that drinking chocolate became fashionable at the French court. Thereafter, by the end of the seventeenth century, it was established elsewhere in Europe – in Germany, Austria and Switzerland.

The drink came to England too in the seventeenth century and chocolate houses began to rival the coffee houses of London. Samuel Pepys records in his *Diary* how, the morning after celebrating rather too well the coronation of Charles II, he was given a cup of chocolate 'to settle my stomach'. The chocolate houses – White's and the Cocoa Tree foremost among them – were popular meeting places for writers until well into the eighteenth century.

In 1724 the Government imposed a heavy duty on chocolate (governments do not change much) and it became the drink of the rich. While it remained so, it was served with style. Special pots, silver or fine china, were made for it, elaborate chocolate 'mills' were designed to whip the drink into a froth that helped to disguise its oiliness. With the reduction of the tax in the early nineteenth century it became a drink for the many, and although some of the mystique may have been lost, the pleasure was spread. But it was still a drink only. The first steps towards transforming it into eating chocolate were to be taken in the nineteenth century in England, the Netherlands and Switzerland, and back across the Atlantic in the USA.

INTRODUCTION

In 1728 the first English factory for processing the cocoa bean was opened in Bristol, and in 1765 a factory was set up in the USA. Chocolate was made at first by grinding the roasted cocoa bean into what was called 'chocolate liquor' and mixing it with sugar and spices. This was then brewed into a thick, rich beverage. There is a large fat content in the cocoa bean, some of which could be extracted by a hand press. Most of it remained in the brew, however, and we today should probably find it most unpalatable. Manufacturers went some way towards counteracting the fat by adding flour, cornmeal, oatmeal, arrowroot and even dried acorns.

In 1828, a Dutchman, Conrad van Houten, invented a press which could extract a large proportion of the fat (cocoa butter) from the bean, leaving a dry, powdery cake. Twenty years later the firm of Joseph Fry, of Bristol, discovered how to combine the cocoa butter with the chocolate liquor and sugar. Eating chocolate was born.

The development of the chocolate industry owes an immense debt to the Quakers. Believing firmly in the virtues of temperance, they eagerly took up the distribution of tea, coffee and cocoa, and later the manufacture of chocolate. It was at this period that the great Quaker families, their names today synonymous with most popular brands of chocolate – the Cadburys, Frys – and Rowntrees – founded their fortunes. With their minds firmly fixed on social reform, they were excellent employers and gave much thought to the welfare of their workers. Up-to-date factories were built and garden suburbs established, like the famous one at Bournville, for their workpeople, and their business prospered.

With the discovery in Switzerland, towards the end of the last century, of the first milk chocolate (made with Nestlé's condensed milk), and Lindt's extra smooth *chocolat fondant*, the scene was set for the great twentieth-century explosion of chocolate in all the forms we know and love today.

The Cocoa Bean

What is it then, this food beloved by all, that has come down to us over the centuries? Chocolate is made from the cocoa bean, the fruit of a tropical tree that flourishes in a belt round the world extending about 20 degrees north and south of the equator. It is believed to be about 4,000 years old, but our first definite knowledge of it comes from the Aztecs of Central America, from about 600 AD.

After the sixteenth-century discovery of the New World, the Spaniards established cocoa plantations in their Central and South American colonies, and in many islands in and around the Caribbean. In the next century the Dutch took cocoa trees east to Indonesia and Ceylon; the trees were later introduced to equatorial Africa and today Nigeria and Ghana are the world's leading cocoa growers, with Brazil in third place.

A crop of cocoa beans is produced by a tree after three or four years, and after ten years the tree is fully mature. It has a useful life of about thirty years, although some have lived as long as 200 years. The tree has large glossy leaves, with waxy white or pink blossoms: these develop into large pods containing the beans. The pods are harvested by skilled pickers using special knives. They are then split open and the beans – between twenty and fifty to a pod – as well as the pulp in which they lie, are scooped out and laid in great piles on the ground to ferment. They are then dried – in the sun or in special drying sheds – before they are shipped to the factory. Here they are cleaned, sorted and blended, then roasted – and each manufacturer has his own procedure for this. After roasting, the beans are cracked to remove the shells and expose the 'nibs' (or kernels). The nibs are then crushed to reduce them to a paste and release the cocoa butter. The result is the substance known as chocolate liquor (which, set, can be used as unsweetened cooking chocolate).

The chocolate liquor can now be made into cocoa powder, in which case it is pressed again to extract more cocoa butter and leave a pure powder. Or it can become eating chocolate by the addition of more cocoa butter, sugar and flavourings and, for milk chocolate, milk. It is then rolled again, refined and smoothed, until it is at last ready to be poured into moulds. Finally it is wrapped by machines and is ready for sale.

The Virtues of Chocolate

Why is chocolate so universally loved? Among its virtues, it is an excellent quick-energy food, containing as it does protein, fat, carbohydrate, calcium, phosphorus, iron, sodium, potassium, Vitamin A, thiamine, riboflavin and niacin. It is easily digested and highly valued as a food by athletes, travellers and all those engaged in hard physical work.

It is most obliging in the kitchen. All cooks know how coffee and chocolate combine to enhance each other, but chocolate takes kindly to the addition of all manner of different flavours. The Aztecs used cinnamon and other spices with it, we add vanilla, mint, orange and other fruits, brandy, rum and liqueurs.

Finally, chocolate may or may not be an aphrodisiac. Controversy has raged over this question down the years, and no very definite conclusion seems to have been reached. One thing is in no doubt, though: chocolate has a powerful magic all of its own.

Types of Chocolate

This is a very brief resumé of the different varieties and types of chocolate and chocolate products.

Plain chocolate
This is a pure chocolate made with cocoa butter, and has little sugar added. It can also be called bitter or dessert chocolate. It is ideal for making rich desserts and puddings when a true chocolate flavour is required.

Milk chocolate
This is a sweet chocolate with a lower cocoa content than plain chocolate. It has additions – of milk, dried or condensed – and the flavour of a dish made with it will not have nearly as rich a chocolate flavour. It will also be very sweet.

Cooking chocolate
This is, as the name implies, sold for cooking purposes. It is not real chocolate,

but has a chocolate flavour. The real cocoa butter found in proper chocolate is replaced by other fats such as coconut oil that alter the melting properties. This applies to chocolate-flavoured cake coverings too.

Chocolate couverture
This is generally only available to professional cooks. It has a high content of cocoa butter, and flows very smoothly when melted.

White chocolate
Nice to eat but not for cooking, as it lacks the essential chocolate colour (because it contains no chocolate liquor).

Cocoa powder
This has no sugar and very little cocoa butter. Cocoa is the most economical method of achieving a good chocolate flavour in cooking. Cocoa contains a proportion of starch and these starch cells need to be broken down. For this reason cocoa powder should be blended with a proportion of boiling water or cooked to obtain a better flavour.

Drinking chocolate
This is cocoa and sugar mixed with a lower proportion of starch than cocoa. It has a milder flavour than cocoa, and is mainly used for drinks as its name suggests.

Chocolate flake
This is made from milk chocolate which is compressed so that thin layers roll against each other forming flakes. These are then cut into lengths. Flakes are often served with ice cream, but can be most useful for cake decorations.

Chocolate buttons
These are made from milk chocolate and are very useful for cake decorations.

Chocolate Tips

The following are a few suggestions to enable you to store, melt and use your delicious chocolate correctly.

Storing chocolate
Chocolate stores well in a cool dark place. Plain chocolate will keep under these conditions for up to a year, and milk chocolate up to six months. Chocolate can be kept in the fridge or freezer, but it may sweat when brought to room temperature, and a whitish film or bloom may develop. This whiteness is due to cocoa butter or sugar crystals rising to the surface and can also occur if chocolate is stored in too warm a place.

Chocolate should be carefully wrapped, as it does pick up odours. I'm sure that most people have had chocolate that tasted of the mint sweets it was stored next to in the sweetshop!

Melting chocolate
First break the chocolate into small pieces and put into a china or oven-glass bowl. Stand the bowl over a pan of very hot water and allow to melt slowly. (Don't do this over a pan of *boiling* water otherwise more than likely the chocolate will go into a thick dark-coloured solid mass and lose its shine.) Remember that chocolate will melt in a child's pocket or on a sunny window sill in summer – a reminder of what a gentle heat is needed.

Adding water to chocolate
Never add water to chocolate when melting it unless the recipe suggests it. If the particular chocolate is too thick it can be thinned down with a little vegetable oil.

Chocolate caraque (curls)
Very easy, but don't use real chocolate, which will just crumble into short flakes: use cooking chocolate (I prefer the plain variety) or chocolate cake covering. Melt as usual, then spread thinly over a marble slab, or laminated top, using a palette knife. Leave to set for a few moments (the time will vary according to the temperature of the kitchen) then, with a French cooks' knife at an angle of 45 degrees, push the knife forward to 'scrape' the chocolate into curls. Store in a plastic container or put straight on top of the cake.

Grated or short chocolate curls
It helps to slightly warm the bar of choco-

late before grating on the coarsest side of the grater. To make short chocolate curls, warm the bar slightly and, using a swivel-bladed potato peeler, thinly shave curls off the back of the chocolate block.

Chocolate leaves

Using unblemished rose leaves, take scant teaspoonfuls of melted chocolate and use to evenly coat the veined sides of the leaves. Arrange on silicone paper and allow to set. When set, carefully peel away and discard the green leaf.

Chocolate shapes

Trace outlines such as leaf shapes, flowers, stars, butterflies and swans on to a sheet of plain white paper. Cover with a piece of silicone paper. Fill a greaseproof paper piping bag with melted chocolate, snip off the tip of the bag and follow the shapes on the paper. Either fill in the centres completely or fill with lattice work. When set, carefully peel off the silicone paper. Keep shapes in a cool dry place as they will soon begin to melt.

Chocolate cut-outs

Spread melted chocolate out thickly on a sheet of silicone paper. Allow to set. Cut out the shapes with small cocktail or aspic cutters. Alternately, cut into even-sized squares and triangles with a sharp knife. Melt remaining chocolate to use again.

CHOCOLATE DESSERTS

Fantastic Chocolate Dessert

SERVES 4

This really is so easy to do, and nobody knows exactly what it is. I always keep fresh white breadcrumbs in the freezer so that they are ready for use in this recipe – as well as in others! I like to make this dessert the day before I am going to serve it.

4 rounded tablespoons drinking chocolate
1 level tablespoon instant coffee powder
4oz (100g) fresh white breadcrumbs
4oz (100g) demerara sugar
½ pt (300ml) whipping cream
chocolate flake, to decorate

Put the chocolate, coffee powder, breadcrumbs and sugar in a bowl and mix thoroughly. Whip the cream with an electric or hand rotary whisk until thick, and soft peaks are formed.

Spread alternate layers of chocolate mixture and cream in 4 white wine glasses, starting with chocolate and finishing with a layer of cream.

Leave in the refrigerator overnight before serving, decorated with the quartered chocolate flake.

Chocolate Whisky Honeycomb Special

SERVES 6

A rich chocolate and whisky flavoured cream, with honeycomb pieces to add a surprise crunch.

about 12 sponge fingers, halved
4oz (100g) butter, softened
4oz (100g) caster sugar
2 eggs, separated
4oz (100g) plain chocolate, broken into small pieces
2 tablespoons whisky
4oz (100g) packet Maltesers
¼ pt (150ml) whipping cream, whipped, to decorate

Line the sides of a 7 inch (17·5cm) round loose-bottomed cake tin with the sponge fingers, sugar side out. This is made easier if you spread the sides of the fingers with a little extra butter so they stick to each other.

Beat together the measured butter and sugar until light and creamy. Beat the egg yolks into the creamed mixture.

Put chocolate in a bowl and allow to melt over a pan of simmering water, then remove from heat. Allow to cool a little. Whisk the egg whites until stiff with an electric or rotary whisk, then fold into the creamed mixture with the chocolate and whisky. Stir in most of the Maltesers, saving a few for decoration.

Turn this mixture into the tin and smooth the top. Chill in the refrigerator overnight. Turn out onto a serving dish and decorate with whipped cream and remaining Maltesers just before serving.

Chocolate and Orange Mousse

SERVES 6–8

This is a lovely refreshing mousse. Chocolate and orange go so well together.

½oz (15g) powdered gelatine
3 tablespoons water
finely grated rind and juice of 1 orange
8oz (225g) plain chocolate, broken into small pieces
5 eggs, separated
4oz (100g) caster sugar
½ pt (300ml) whipping cream, whipped

Put the gelatine in a small bowl with the water, orange rind and juice. Leave to stand for about 3 minutes to form a sponge. Stand the bowl over a pan of simmering water until gelatine has dissolved.

Put chocolate in a bowl and stand over a pan of gently simmering water until melted. Remove from the heat, cool slightly, then stir in the egg yolks. Stir the gelatine into the chocolate and leave to cool but not set.

Whisk the egg whites with a small electric whisk until frothy then add the sugar a teaspoonful at a time, whisking well after each addition. Quickly fold in the chocolate mixture and then stir in half the whipped cream.

Divide between 6–8 individual glass dishes and chill until set. Decorate with swirls of the remaining cream just before serving.

Ursula MacKenzie's Chocolate Pots

MAKES 4–6

When you add the pieces of chocolate to the hot cream, the chocolate will melt and form flecks in the cream. After processing, however, it will be lovely and smooth. It's a really delicious dessert.

½ pt (300ml) single cream
6oz (175g) plain chocolate, broken into small pieces
1 egg, separated
1 tablespoon Cointreau
a little grated chocolate, to decorate

Put the cream in a pan and heat gently to boiling point. Remove from the heat, add chocolate pieces and stir until chocolate has melted.

Pour chocolate mixture into a processor or blender and process for a few seconds. Add egg yolk and Cointreau then process until well blended.

Whisk egg white with an electric or rotary whisk until it forms soft peaks, then fold chocolate mixture into it. Divide the mixture between 4–6 small ramekin dishes, and chill well before serving.

Decorate with a little grated chocolate sprinkled on top.

Chocolate Cups with Lime Mousse

MAKES ABOUT 12

A particular favourite with children. Lemon mousse can be used instead of lime if limes are difficult to obtain.

6oz (175g) plain chocolate, broken into small pieces
½oz (15g) butter

FOR THE MOUSSE
2 eggs, separated
2oz (50g) caster sugar
finely grated rind and juice of 1 large lime
½oz (15g) gelatine
3 tablespoons cold water

Put the chocolate and butter in a bowl and stand over a pan of gently simmering water until melted. Remove from the heat and use to line the insides of about 12 waxed paper cases. Spread the chocolate around the base and sides of each case using the handle of a teaspoon to make a smooth coating. Put the cases in the refrigerator to set, then carefully peel off paper cases.

Meanwhile prepare the mousse. Put the egg yolks in a bowl with the sugar, and beat well until light and creamy. Put the whites in a larger bowl ready for whisking. Stir the lime rind and juice into the yolk mixture.

Put the gelatine and water in a small bowl and leave to stand for about 3 minutes to form a sponge. Stand the bowl over a pan of simmering water until dissolved. Cool slightly then stir into the yolk mixture. Leave to cool but not set.

Whisk the egg whites, using a rotary or small electric hand whisk, until stiff then fold into the lime mixture. Divide mousse between the chocolate cases and chill in the refrigerator until set.

Chocolate and Cherry Mousse

SERVES 4–6

Serve this deliciously rich mousse really well chilled.

15oz (425g) can stoned black cherries
1oz (25g) powdered gelatine (2 packets)
6 tablespoons cold water
3 eggs, separated
2oz (50g) caster sugar, warmed
4oz (100g) plain chocolate, broken into small pieces
3 tablespoons Kirsch
½ pt (300ml) double cream

Drain cherries, reserve 3 for decoration, then purée the remainder in a processor or blender.

Put the gelatine in a small bowl with the water and allow to stand for 3 minutes to form a sponge. Stand bowl over a pan of simmering water until dissolved, then remove from heat and allow to cool slightly.

Put the egg whites in a large bowl and the yolks in a smaller bowl with the sugar. Whisk yolks until pale and creamy. Melt chocolate in a bowl over a pan of simmering water, remove from heat and stir in the Kirsch, cherries and egg yolk mixture. Whip half the cream and fold it in gently, then whisk the egg whites with a rotary or electric whisk until they form peaks. Stir these too into the chocolate mixture.

Turn the mixture into a 1 pint (600ml) soufflé dish and chill in the refrigerator until set. To set, decorate with remaining whipped cream and the reserved cherries.

Chocolate and Banana Cream

SERVES 4–6

The banana gives a really fruity flavour to this dessert. Chocolate and banana are such a good combination, and it's very easy to prepare.

4oz (100g) plain chocolate, broken into small pieces
½ pt (300ml) whipping cream
2 large bananas
2 tablespoons sherry

Put 2 squares of chocolate to one side, and melt remaining chocolate slowly in a bowl over a pan of simmering water. Remove from heat and allow to cool slightly.

Whisk cream in a bowl until it stands in peaks. Peel the bananas, and mash them on a plate with a fork. Fold them, along with the chocolate and sherry, into the cream. Divide the mixture between 4–6 serving glasses.

Grate the reserved chocolate and sprinkle a little on the top of each dessert to decorate. Chill well before serving.

Everlasting Brandy Syllabub

SERVES 4–6

A rather luxurious sweet to serve for a dinner party. It is simple to make and lends itself to spectacular variations.

finely grated rind and juice of 1 lemon
3oz (75g) caster sugar
2 tablespoons brandy
2 tablespoons sweet sherry
½ pt (300ml) double cream, whipped
3oz (75g) plain chocolate, coarsely grated

Put the lemon rind, juice, sugar, brandy and sherry in a bowl and chill in the refrigerator for about 3 hours until the rind has softened.

Stir lemon mixture into the whipped cream with the grated chocolate. Divide between 4–6 glasses and serve well chilled.

Kiwi Syllabub
For a really spectacular dessert, peel and slice 2 kiwi fruits and use to line 4–6 tall glasses before spooning the syllabub in the middle. Chill well before serving.

Coffee and Orange Syllabub
Omit the lemon juice and rind and add 2 tablespoons coffee essence and the grated rind and juice of 1 small orange instead.

Chocolate Trifle

SERVES 6

This family pudding is a particular favourite with children, and is so easy to prepare. If you have no pears, then pineapple is just as delicious.

1 chocolate Swiss roll
14oz (397g) can pear halves
3 tablespoons custard powder
3 tablespoons cocoa
3 tablespoons caster sugar
1 pt (600ml) milk
¼ pt (150ml) whipping cream
chocolate vermicelli or grated chocolate, to decorate

Cut the Swiss roll into 8 slices and arrange in the bottom of a 2 pint (1·2 litre) glass serving dish. Pour juice from pears over this, then halve the pears and arrange on top.

Mix custard powder, cocoa and sugar to a smooth paste with a little of the milk. Bring remaining milk to the boil and pour onto paste, stirring well. Return to pan and bring back to the boil, stirring until thickened. Remove from heat and allow to cool with a piece of damp greaseproof paper over the custard to prevent a skin forming. When cold, beat well, or process in a processor or blender until light and creamy then pour over fruit and leave to set.

Whisk the whipping cream until it is stiff and forms soft peaks, then spread over trifle and sprinkle with vermicelli or grated chocolate just before serving.

Chocolate Mousse Trifle

SERVES 8

Very rich and wicked! Serve it after a light main course.

6oz (175g) plain chocolate, broken into small pieces
2 teaspoons instant coffee powder
4 tablespoons cold water
1oz (25g) butter
3 eggs, separated
4 tablespoons inexpensive sherry
1oz (25g) caster sugar
1 packet sponge fingers
whipped cream, to decorate

Put the chocolate with the coffee and water in a bowl and allow to dissolve over a pan of simmering water. Add butter, then remove from heat and allow to cool slightly before beating in egg yolks and 1 tablespoon sherry.

Whisk egg whites in a separate bowl with an electric whisk until they form peaks then whisk in sugar a teaspoonful at a time, beating well after each addition. Gently fold chocolate mixture into whites until thoroughly mixed, then stand on one side.

Arrange sponge fingers in the bottom of a 2 pint (1·2 litre) shallow glass bowl, pour remaining sherry over them, then top with chocolate mixture. Leave to set in the refrigerator for about 4 hours. Decorate with cream.

Chocolate Charlotte

SERVES 8

A really lovely dessert, but it's rich, so serve in thin slices. For a special occasion use gold almonds for decoration; otherwise chocolate drops or Maltesers will do.

3 tablespoons brandy
28 sponge fingers (about 1 packet)

FOR THE MOUSSE
4oz (100g) plain chocolate, broken into small pieces
6oz (175g) unsalted butter
5oz (150g) caster sugar
2 eggs, separated

TO DECORATE
a little whipped cream
gold almonds or chocolate drops

Line a 2lb (1kg) loaf tin with foil. Put brandy in a flattish soup plate. Dip each sponge finger, sponge side down, into the brandy and arrange 9 or 10 sugar side down on the base of the tin. Cut the remainder in half. Dip in the brandy and stand up around the inside of the tin.

Now prepare the mousse. Put the chocolate in a bowl over a pan of simmering water and allow to melt. Cream the butter, sugar and egg yolks really well in a bowl until creamy – or process in a processor or blender – then stir in the cool but still runny melted chocolate. Whisk the egg whites until stiff, using a rotary or small electric hand whisk, then fold into the chocolate mixture.

Turn into the loaf tin and chill in the refrigerator overnight. Turn out onto a serving dish, peel off the foil and decorate with the whipped cream and almonds or chocolate drops.

Chocolate Cream Charlotte

SERVES 8

This Chocolate Cream Charlotte is quite tricky to make, but delicious.

2oz (50g) caster sugar, warmed
3 eggs
4oz (100g) plain chocolate, broken into small pieces
½oz (15g) powdered gelatine
4 tablespoons cold water
½ pt (300ml) double cream
3 tablespoons orange juice
3 tablespoons rum
28 sponge fingers (about 1 packet)

TO DECORATE
¼ pt (150ml) whipping cream, whipped
1oz (25g) flaked almonds, toasted

Put the sugar and eggs in a bowl and whisk on highest speed with an electric or rotary whisk until stiff enough to leave a trail.

Put the chocolate in a bowl and stand over a pan of simmering water until melted. Put the gelatine and water in a small bowl and leave to stand for about 3 minutes to form a sponge, then stand in a pan of simmering water until dissolved. Remove from heat and allow to cool.

Whisk the cream until it holds soft peaks then stir in the chocolate and gelatine. Fold this mixture into the eggs and sugar.

Mix orange juice and rum in a flattish dish. Dip the unsugared side of the sponge fingers into this and arrange sugar side out in an 8 inch (20cm) round deep cake tin to form a circle around the side. Pour chocolate mixture into the centre. Chill in the refrigerator until set.

To serve, dip the tin quickly in hot water and turn out onto a serving dish and decorate with whipped cream and toasted almonds.

Chocolate and Praline Bombe

SERVES 10–12

An impressive rich chocolate dessert with crunchy pieces of praline.

FOR THE PRALINE
4oz (100g) caster sugar
⅛ pt (75ml) water
2oz (50g) blanched almonds

FOR THE BOMBE
12oz (350g) plain chocolate, broken into small pieces
3oz (75g) unsalted butter 2 tablespoons rum
½ pt (300ml) whipping cream

chocolate squares or buttons, to decorate

First make the praline. Dissolve sugar in water in a strong pan over a low heat, then boil rapidly until a pale caramel colour. This takes about 10 minutes. Scatter the almonds on a sheet of silicone paper, pour caramel over almonds, then leave to harden.

To make the bombe, put chocolate in a bowl over a pan of simmering water until melted. Cream butter in a bowl, add chocolate and rum, and beat well. Stir in the crushed praline.

Lightly grease a 1 pt (600ml) bombe mould or oven-glass basin. Lightly whip three-quarters of the cream until it stands in peaks then gently fold it into the chocolate mixture (saving the rest for decoration). Turn mixture into the prepared basin and refrigerate overnight.

Turn the bombe out onto a serving dish by quickly dipping the bowl into very hot water for a couple of seconds, and then turning out. (If it hasn't turned out perfectly then smooth it over with a palette knife.) Pipe swirls of cream around the base, topping every other one with a chocolate square or button. Serve chilled, sliced in wedges.

Chocolate Juliette

SERVES 8–10

A very rich sweet, so serve in thin slices – they can always come back for second helpings.

8oz (225g) milk chocolate, broken into small pieces
8oz (225g) hard margarine
2 eggs
1oz (25g) caster sugar
8oz (225g) 'Nice' biscuits
1oz (25g) glacé cherries, chopped
1oz (25g) almonds, chopped

TO DECORATE
¼ pt (150ml) double cream, whipped
chocolate buttons or matchsticks

Line a small 7½ × 4 × 2½ inch (19 × 10 × 6cm) loaf tin with foil.

Put the chocolate in a pan with the margarine, and heat gently until melted. Beat the eggs and sugar together until blended, then gradually add the chocolate mixture, a little at a time.

Break the biscuits into ½ inch (1·25cm) pieces, and stir into the chocolate mixture with the glacé cherries and chopped nuts. Pack into the tin and smooth the top. Leave to set in the refrigerator overnight until firm.

Turn out onto a serving dish and peel off the foil. Decorate with the cream and chocolate buttons or matchsticks.

Rum and Raisin Chocolate Cheesecake

SERVES 10

This takes time to make but is well worth it for a special occasion. The crumb base is made in the conventional way: put the biscuits into a plastic bag and crush them to crumbs with a rolling pin. The cheesecake filling is extra delicious, and the rum-soaked raisins are a boozy and unexpected taste sensation.

2oz (50g) raisins
4 tablespoons rum

FOR THE CRUST

2½oz (65g) butter
2oz (50g) demerara sugar
5oz (150g) digestive biscuits, made into crumbs

FOR THE CHEESECAKE

1 teaspoon instant coffee powder
2 level tablespoons cocoa, sieved
3 tablespoons boiling water
2 eggs, separated
2oz (50g) caster sugar
½oz (15g) packet powdered gelatine
3 tablespoons cold water
8oz (225g) cream cheese
¼ pt (150ml) whipping cream, lightly whipped

TO DECORATE

¼ pt (150ml) whipping cream, whipped
chocolate flake or drops

Soak the raisins in the rum overnight.

To make the crumb crust, melt the butter in a pan and stir in the sugar and biscuit crumbs until well blended. Press over sides and base of a 9 inch (22·5cm) flan dish. Put in the refrigerator to harden.

Meanwhile prepare the cheesecake filling. Mix the coffee and cocoa in a bowl with the boiling water, then add the egg yolks and sugar. Stand the bowl over a pan of simmering water and stir until the mixture will coat the back of the spoon. This takes about 10 minutes.

Mix gelatine and cold water in a bowl and leave to stand for about 3 minutes to form a sponge. Place bowl over a pan of simmering water, and dissolve gelatine until quite clear. Remove from the heat, allow to cool slightly, then stir into the coffee and cocoa mixture.

In a large bowl, beat the cream cheese until soft, then gradually stir in the cooled coffee and cocoa mixture and the whipped cream. Add the rum and raisins and pour the mixture into the flan case. Put in the refrigerator until set.

Decorate with the whipped cream and chocolate flake or drops, and serve cut in wedges.

Chocolate Fudge Flan

SERVES 6–8

A delicious fudge mixture in a biscuit flan. Fattening – but worth it!

2oz (50g) butter
1oz (25g) demerara sugar
4oz (100g) digestive biscuits, made into crumbs

FOR THE FILLING
10oz (275g) light muscovado sugar
¼ pt (150ml) water
2oz (50g) unsalted butter
2oz (50g) mixed nuts, chopped
¼ pt (150ml) double cream
2oz (50g) plain chocolate

Melt the butter in a pan then remove from heat and stir in the sugar and biscuit crumbs. Mix well until thoroughly coated then turn mixture into an 8 inch (20cm) fluted flan tin. Press onto the sides and base of the tin with the back of a spoon.

For the filling, put sugar and water in a pan and heat over a low heat until sugar has dissolved. Bring to the boil and simmer without stirring until it becomes a straw-coloured caramel. Remove from the heat, carefully add the butter, and stir until smooth. Add the nuts and all but 1 dessertspoon of the cream. Return to the heat and gently bring to the boil then simmer for about 10 minutes until the mixture has thickened. Remove from the heat, allow to cool a little then pour into crumb base.

Melt chocolate in a bowl over a pan of simmering water. Once melted, stir in the remaining cream then spread over the fudge filling. Chill in the refrigerator for about 2 hours before serving in wedges, with pouring cream if liked.

Chocolate Sundaes

SERVES 4

These are quick to prepare and a good standby when unexpected guests arrive for supper. I use whichever canned fruits I happen to have in the cupboard although the fruits in natural syrup are so much nicer than those in the heavy sweet syrups.

8 sponge fingers
3 tablespoons rum
15oz (425g) can pear halves
chocolate chip ice cream (see page 38)
¼ pt (150ml) whipping cream, whipped
chocolate sauce (see page 90)
2oz (50g) chopped walnuts

Soak the sponge fingers in the rum and divide between 4 sundae dishes or tall glasses.

Drain the pears and chop roughly then arrange on top of the sponge fingers.

Spoon a generous scoopful of ice cream on top of the pears and then pipe a blob of cream on top of this. Pour over a little chocolate sauce and sprinkle with chopped nuts. Serve straightaway.

Frozen Chocolate Mousse Pots

SERVES 6–8

This is an excellent way of using up egg whites which you may have left over after making mayonnaise. It's light, tasty, and an unusual ice cream to serve.

4oz (100g) plain chocolate, broken into small pieces
1 level tablespoon cocoa, sieved
1 level teaspoon instant coffee powder
2 tablespoons hot water
6 egg whites
3oz (75g) caster sugar

Put the chocolate in a bowl and stand over a pan of gently simmering water until melted. Mix the cocoa, coffee and water, then stir into the melted chocolate and beat well until thick and creamy.

Whisk the egg whites until stiff then gradually add the sugar a teaspoonful at a time, whisking well after each addition. Fold in the chocolate mixture until thoroughly blended.

Divide the mixture between 6–8 ramekin dishes. Store in the freezer for up to 10 days. Serve still frozen with a little single cream.

Chocolate Mint Ice Cream

SERVES 8–10

A rich ice cream that needs no rewhisking during freezing – which makes it extra easy to prepare. It is light and mousse-like after freezing.

4 eggs, separated
4oz (100g) caster sugar
½ pt (300ml) whipping cream
3oz (75g) mint chocolate matchsticks, broken
3–6 drops peppermint essence (to taste)
about 6 drops green food colouring

Put the egg yolks in a small bowl and whisk until well blended. In a larger bowl whisk the egg whites with an electric or rotary whisk until stiff, then whisk in the sugar a teaspoonful at a time.

Whisk the cream until it forms soft peaks, then fold into egg whites with the yolks, broken chocolate matchsticks, peppermint essence and food colouring (just enough to give a light green colour). Mix thoroughly.

Turn into a 2½ pint (1·4 litre) shallow container, cover and freeze until solid, ideally overnight. Remove from freezer and stand at room temperature for about 5–10 minutes before serving.

Children's Chocolate Ice Cream

SERVES 8

The cocoa in this recipe gives the ice cream a rich chocolate flavour, and using evaporated milk makes it inexpensive to prepare. It doesn't need rewhisking during freezing, so is easy enough for the children to make themselves!

1oz (25g) cocoa
4 tablespoons boiling water
4 eggs, separated
5oz (150g) caster sugar
14½oz (410g) can evaporated milk, chilled overnight

Put the cocoa in a small bowl with the water and stir until well blended and smooth. Leave to cool then beat in the egg yolks. Whisk the egg whites with an electric or rotary hand whisk on high speed until they are stiff, then whisk in the sugar a teaspoonful at a time.

Whisk the evaporated milk until it just holds soft peaks, then fold it into the egg whites together with the chocolate mixture. Turn into a 3½ pint (2·1 litre) rigid container. Cover, label and freeze, then use as required.

Leave to thaw at room temperature for 5–10 minutes, then serve in scoops in individual dishes.

Chocolate and Rum Ice Cream

SERVES 8

This is a rich and boozy ice cream, with a really chocolatey and rummy flavour.

1½oz (40g) cocoa, sieved
2 tablespoons hot water
3oz (75g) plain chocolate, broken into small pieces
2 tablespoons rum
4 eggs, separated
4oz (100g) caster sugar
½ pt (300ml) double cream

Measure cocoa into a small bowl, and mix to a paste with the hot water. Add the chocolate, and put the bowl over a pan of simmering water. Leave until the chocolate has melted, then stir in the rum.

Put the egg yolks in a small bowl and stir until well blended. Whisk the egg whites until stiff, whisking in the sugar a tablespoonful at a time.

Whisk the cream until it forms soft peaks. Add the chocolate mixture to the egg yolks and then fold this into the egg whites with the cream.

Turn the completed ice cream into a 2½ pint (1·4 litre) container – old shallow ice cream cartons are good. Cover and freeze until solid, ideally overnight. Before serving, remove from the freezer and leave at room temperature for about 5–10 minutes.

Chocolate Chip Ice Cream

SERVES 10–12

It is possible to buy chocolate chips but I think it is far nicer to add mint chocolates – without the soft centre – which can be broken up and then stirred into the ice cream mixture. Alternatively add some broken-up seaside rock.

½ pt (300ml) double cream
1 pt (600ml) milk
12oz (350g) caster sugar
a few drops vanilla essence
2oz (50g) chocolate mints or mint cracknel, broken

Pour the cream into a large mixing bowl, whisk until it forms soft peaks then stir in the milk, sugar, vanilla essence and broken chocolate until evenly blended. Pour this mixture into a 2½ pint (1·4 litre) container, cover with a lid and freeze for about 6 hours until firm.

Take the frozen mixture from the freezer, turn into a large mixing bowl and break up slightly, then either process in a processor or whisk with an electric whisk until smooth and creamy. Return to the container and freeze until required. Serve in scoops.

Chocolate Baked Alaska

SERVES 4–6

This is a top favourite for birthdays and parties. Once assembled, it can be kept in the freezer for up to 1 week and then browned in the oven. Although most people think it difficult, it is really very easy, and is *always* well appreciated!

1 chocolate Swiss roll, bought or home-made
2 tablespoons brandy
about 10 scoops chocolate ice cream
2 egg whites
4oz (100g) caster sugar

Heat the oven to 450°F/230°C/Gas Mark 8.

Slice the Swiss roll into 8 slices and arrange close together on an 8 inch (20cm) ovenproof plate. Sprinkle with brandy. Pile scoops of ice cream on top of the Swiss roll then put in the freezer whilst preparing the meringue.

Whisk egg whites until stiff then whisk in sugar a teaspoonful at a time until all is incorporated. Take ice cream out of freezer and spread meringue all over the ice cream so it is completely sealed.

Bake in the oven for about 3 minutes until meringue is tinged a pale golden brown. Serve immediately.

Hot Chocolate Pudding with Chocolate Sauce

SERVES 4

A hot chocolate pudding covered with hot chocolate sauce is perfect for a cold winter's day.

FOR THE PUDDING

4oz (100g) soft margarine
4oz (100g) caster sugar
2 eggs
3½oz (90g) self-raising flour
1oz (25g) cocoa, sieved
1 level teaspoon baking powder
3 tablespoons milk

FOR THE SAUCE

¾ pt (450ml) water
1oz (25g) cocoa, sieved
1½oz (40g) custard powder
3oz (75g) granulated sugar

Heat the oven to 350°F/180°C/Gas Mark 4, and lightly butter a 1¼ pint (750ml) ovenproof dish.

Put all the ingredients for the pudding in a bowl and beat well for about 2 minutes until well blended. Turn into the prepared dish and bake in the oven for about 45 minutes until well risen and firm to the touch.

Meanwhile prepare the sauce. Mix 5 tablespoons of the water with the cocoa and custard powder in a bowl. Bring the remainder of the water to the boil with the sugar, stirring until dissolved. Remove from heat and mix gradually into the cocoa mixture. Return the sauce to the pan stirring all the time until thickened. Serve hot sauce poured over slices of the pudding.

Hot Chocolate Soufflé

SERVES 4

So delicious and yet quite simple to make. It's best served with whipped cream.

4oz (100g) plain chocolate, broken into small pieces
2 tablespoons water
½ pt (300ml) milk
1½oz (40g) butter
1½oz (40g) flour
1 teaspoon vanilla essence
4 large eggs, separated
2oz (50g) caster sugar
a little icing sugar, to decorate

Heat the oven to 375°F/190°C/Gas Mark 5 and place a baking sheet in it.

Melt the chocolate in a pan with the water and 2 tablespoons of the milk. Keep stirring until the chocolate has melted. Add the remaining milk, bring to the boil then remove from the heat.

Melt the butter in a small pan, stir in the flour, and cook for 2 minutes without browning. Remove from the heat and stir in the hot chocolate milk. Return to the heat, stirring until thickened. Stir in the vanilla essence then allow to cool.

Beat the egg yolks one at a time into the chocolate sauce, then sprinkle on the sugar. Whisk the egg whites, using a rotary or small electric whisk, until stiff but not dry. Stir 1 tablespoonful into the chocolate sauce then fold in the remainder. Pour into a buttered 2 pint (1·2 litre) soufflé dish, and bake in the oven on the hot baking sheet for about 40 minutes. Sprinkle with icing sugar then serve immediately.

Chocolate Upside-Down Pudding

SERVES 4–6

Makes a pleasant change from the traditional upside-down pudding.

FOR THE SPONGE

2oz (50g) self-raising flour
1oz (25g) cocoa, sieved
3oz (75g) soft margarine
3oz (75g) caster sugar
1 egg, beaten
1 tablespoon pear juice (from can)
½ level teaspoon baking powder

FOR THE TOPPING

14oz (397g) can pear halves, drained
2–3 glacé cherries, halved
2oz (50g) demerara sugar

Heat the oven to 375°F/190°C/Gas Mark 5. Well butter a 7 inch (17·5cm) deep round cake tin.

Put all the sponge ingredients in a bowl and beat well for about 2 minutes until well blended.

Arrange the pear halves in the base of the buttered tin, first putting a cherry in the cavity in each half of pear so that the cherries are touching the base of the tin. Sprinkle over the sugar. Spread sponge mixture over pears and smooth the top.

Bake in the oven for about 35 minutes until the cake is well risen and springs back when lightly pressed with a finger. Leave to cool in the tin for about 10 minutes then turn out onto a warm serving dish, pears uppermost. Serve warm.

Chocolate Roulade

SERVES 8

This is a French classic. *Expect* it to crack when you roll it up.

6 large eggs, separated
5oz (150g) caster sugar
2oz (50g) cocoa
2 tablespoons boiling water

FOR THE FILLING
Icing sugar
¼–½ pt (150–300ml) whipping cream
2 tablespoons brandy

Heat the oven to 350°F/180°C/Gas Mark 4. Grease and line a 12 × 8 inch (30 × 20cm) Swiss roll tin with greaseproof paper.

Put the egg whites in a larger bowl and yolks in a smaller bowl. Add caster sugar, cocoa and the boiling water to the yolks and whisk until thick and creamy. Whisk egg whites until stiff but not dry. Add 2 tablespoons of whisked egg whites to the yolk mixture and mix together. Add yolk mixture to the whisked egg whites and fold in with a metal spoon until the mixture is an even colour. Pour the roulade mixture gently into the prepared tin.

Bake in the oven for about 20 minutes until the top is firm. Take the roulade out of the oven, cover with a teatowel and cool for a few hours.

Spread a sheet of greaseproof paper on a work surface and dust heavily with icing sugar. Turn the roulade out on to this and remove the greaseproof paper lining.

Whip the cream until quite stiff, gradually adding the brandy. Spread the cream over the roulade and dust with icing sugar. Confidently roll up the roulade like a Swiss roll. It is *supposed* to crack! Turn onto a marble slab or long serving plate to serve. Dust with yet more icing sugar and keep in the refrigerator until ready to serve.

Chocolate Profiteroles

SERVES ABOUT 6

These are so delicious and look very impressive too. You could make this same choux pastry into éclairs – pipe them into 12 éclair shapes, about 5–6 inches (12·5–15cm) long – and bake them similarly. They are delicious filled with cream and topped with the Chocolate Eclair Icing – which stays beautifully shiny and tastes wonderful.

2oz (50g) butter
¼ pt (150ml) water
2½oz (65g) plain flour, sieved
2 eggs, beaten

FOR THE FILLING
½ pt (300ml) whipping cream, whipped

FOR THE ICING
1½oz (40g) butter
1oz (25g) cocoa, sieved
4oz (100g) icing sugar, sieved
3–4 tablespoons evaporated milk

Heat the oven to 425°F/220°C/Gas Mark 7. Lightly grease a baking sheet.

For the choux pastry, put the butter and water in a small pan, bring to the boil slowly, and allow the butter to melt. Remove from the heat, add the flour all at once, and beat until it forms a soft ball. Gradually beat in the eggs, a little at a time, to make a smooth shiny paste. Put the mixture into a piping bag fitted with a ½ inch (1·25cm) plain nozzle, and pipe into about 20 blobs on the baking sheet, leaving a little room for them to spread.

Bake in the oven for about 10 minutes then reduce the heat to 375°F/190°C/Gas Mark 5, and cook for a further 15–20 minutes until well risen and golden brown. Remove from the oven and split one side of each bun to allow the steam to escape. Cool on a wire rack. Fill each profiterole with the cream.

For the icing, melt the butter in a small pan, stir in the cocoa, then cook gently for a minute. Remove from the heat and stir in the icing sugar and evaporated milk. Beat well until starting to thicken. Dip each cream-filled bun into the icing to cover the top, and leave on one side to set. Pile them up in a pyramid, and serve the same day.

Chocolate Eclair Icing

ENOUGH FOR 12 ÉCLAIRS

2oz (50g) plain chocolate, broken into small pieces
2 tablespoons water
½oz (15g) butter
3oz (75g) icing sugar, sieved

Put the chocolate, water and butter in a bowl and heat gently over a pan of simmering water until the mixture has melted. Remove from the heat and beat in the sugar until smooth. Pour the chocolate sauce into a shallow dish then dip each éclair into the sauce to coat the top. Allow to set, then serve neatly arranged on a serving dish.

Chocolate Pancakes

MAKES 8–10 PANCAKES

These are a delicious alternative to classic pancakes, with cocoa added to the basic batter. They are filled with whipped cream, and served with a chocolate fudge sauce over the top.

FOR THE PANCAKES

caster sugar
3½oz (90g) plain flour
½oz (15g) cocoa, sieved
1 egg
½ pt (300ml) milk and water mixed, half and half
oil

CHOCOLATE FUDGE SAUCE

1½oz (40g) butter
1oz (25g) cocoa, sieved
2–3 tablespoons milk
4oz (100g) icing sugar, sieved

FOR THE FILLING

¼–½ pt (150–300ml) whipping cream, whipped

Sprinkle a little caster sugar onto a sheet of greaseproof paper and put to one side.

To make pancakes, sieve flour and cocoa into a mixing bowl, and make a well in the centre. Add the egg and about half the milk and water. Mix until smooth with a hand whisk, and then blend in remaining milk and water.

Heat an 8 inch (20cm) frying pan with a little oil. When hot wipe off excess oil with kitchen paper. Spoon about 2 tablespoons of the batter into the pan. Tip the pan from side to side so the batter spreads out evenly covering the base. Cook for about a minute until it goes a lighter brown underneath. Turn the pancake over with a palette knife – or toss if you are feeling brave! Cook for another minute until pale.

Slide the pancake out of the pan onto the piece of greaseproof paper and then roll the pancake up. Place this on a hot serving dish over a steaming pan to keep warm. Make the remaining pancakes in the same way, using a little more sugar if necessary.

To make the fudge sauce, melt the butter in a small saucepan, stir in the cocoa and cook gently for 1 minute. Remove from the heat, add milk and icing sugar, and beat well until smooth. You may need to add a little extra milk if you prefer a thinner sauce.

Serve the pancakes with whipped cream in the middle, folded like crêpes in quarters or rolled up. Pour the fudge sauce over them.

FAMILY CAKES AND BISCUITS

Chocolate Victoria Sandwich

Made by the all-in-one method, this cake is a standby in any kitchen.

1 rounded tablespoon cocoa, sieved
2 tablespoons hot water
4oz (100g) soft margarine
4oz (100g) caster sugar
2 large eggs, beaten
3½oz (90g) self-raising flour
1 level teaspoon baking powder

TOPPING AND FILLING
3oz (75g) soft margarine
8oz (225g) icing sugar, sieved
a little coarsely grated milk chocolate, to decorate

Heat the oven to 350°F/180°C/Gas Mark 4. Grease and line with greased greaseproof paper 2 × 7 inch (17·5cm) sandwich tins.

Blend the cocoa and water in a bowl, allow to cool slightly then add margarine, sugar, eggs, flour and baking powder. Beat well for about 2 minutes until smooth. Divide mixture between prepared tins. Smooth the top and bake in the oven for about 25 minutes until sponges spring back when lightly pressed with the finger. Turn sponges out onto a wire rack to cool, removing the paper.

Blend the margarine and sugar until light and creamy then use to sandwich the cakes together and to cover the top. Decorate with grated chocolate.

Chocolate Swiss Roll

It doesn't take long to make a Swiss roll, and if you make sure you weigh the ingredients accurately, then they turn out a treat. This can be used as the basis of many other recipes throughout the book, and it can be transformed into a magnificent Christmas log cake.

3 size 2 eggs
3oz (75g) caster sugar
2oz (50g) self-raising flour, sieved
1oz (25g) cocoa, sieved

FOR THE FILLING
caster sugar
½ pt (300ml) whipping cream, whipped

Heat the oven to 425°F/220°C/Gas Mark 7, and grease and line with greased greaseproof paper a Swiss roll tin, 13 × 9 inches (32·5 × 22·5cm).

Whisk the eggs and sugar together in a large bowl until the mixture is light and creamy and the whisk will leave a trail when lifted out. Add the flour and cocoa and carefully fold it, with a metal spoon, into the mixture.

Turn the mixture into the tin and smooth level with the back of the spoon, making sure it is spread evenly into the corners. Bake in the oven for about 10 minutes until the sponge begins to shrink back from the sides of the tin.

While the cake is cooking, cut out a piece of greaseproof paper a little bigger than the tin and sprinkle it with caster sugar. Invert the cake on to the sugared paper. Quickly loosen the paper on the bottom of the cake and peel it off. To make rolling easier, trim all four edges of the sponge and make a score mark all the way across, 1 inch (2·5cm) in from the rolling edge, being careful not to cut right through. Place another clean piece of greaseproof paper over the cake and roll up with the greaseproof inside. When cold, unroll the Swiss roll, and spread the cake with the cream, taking it almost to the edges then re-roll. Lift the Swiss roll onto a serving dish and serve sprinkled with a little more caster sugar.

Chocolate Log

1 chocolate Swiss roll
4oz (100g) butter, softened
8oz (225g) icing sugar, sieved
2oz (50g) drinking chocolate
a little sieved icing sugar, to decorate

Stand the Swiss roll on a serving plate. For the icing, put the butter, sugar and drinking chocolate into a bowl and beat well until smooth and well blended. Spread evenly over the Swiss roll and rough up with a fork to give the appearance of a log. Dredge with a little sieved icing sugar and decorate with seasonal novelties – tiny robins or Christmas trees.

Chocolate Walnut Cake

Always a favourite to have in the cake tin.

4oz (100g) soft margarine
4oz (100g) light muscovado sugar
2 eggs
4oz (100g) plain flour
2oz (50g) drinking chocolate
1 level teaspoon baking powder
2oz (50g) walnuts, chopped
2 teaspoons coffee essence
4oz (100g) plain chocolate
icing sugar

Heat the oven to 350°F/180°C/Gas Mark 4. Grease and line with greased greaseproof paper the base of an 8 inch (20cm) cake tin.

Cream the margarine and sugar together, then beat in the eggs, one at a time. Sieve the dry ingredients together and fold in with the nuts and coffee essence.

Cut each square of chocolate into 4 pieces and fold through the cake. Turn into the tin and bake in the oven for about 45 minutes, until the cake is well risen and springs back when lightly pressed with a finger. Turn out, remove paper and leave to cool on a wire rack. Dredge with icing sugar before serving.

Chocolate Mocha Cake

Cocoa gives the strongest chocolate flavour and is cheaper to use than plain chocolate.

1oz (25g) cocoa, sieved
2 tablespoons hot water
4oz (100g) soft margarine
4oz (100g) caster sugar
2 large eggs
4oz (100g) self-raising flour
1 level teaspoon baking powder

FOR THE ICING
3oz (75g) soft margarine
8oz (225g) icing sugar, sieved
1 tablespoon milk
1 tablespoon coffee essence

chocolate flake or grated chocolate, to decorate

Heat the oven to 350°F/180°C/Gas Mark 4. Grease and line with greased greaseproof paper 2 × 7 inch (17·5cm) round sandwich tins.

Blend the cocoa with the water in a large bowl. Cool slightly then add the remaining cake ingredients and beat well for 2 minutes until the mixture is thoroughly blended. Turn into the tins and then bake in the oven for about 25 minutes until the cake springs back when lightly pressed with a finger. Turn out, remove paper and leave to cool on a wire rack.

For the icing, put the margarine, icing sugar, milk and coffee essence in a bowl and beat until smooth. Spread one third of this mixture onto 1 cake and put the other cake on top. Cover top with remaining icing and mark attractively with a palette knife. Decorate the top with broken chocolate flake or grated chocolate.

Chocolate and Orange Marble Cake

Not a rich cake but a good family cake for the weekend.

6oz (175g) soft margarine
6oz (175g) caster sugar
6oz (175g) self-raising flour
3 eggs
1 level teaspoon baking powder
1oz (25g) cocoa, sieved
1 tablespoon milk
grated rind and juice of 1 orange

Heat the oven to 350°F/180°C/Gas Mark 4. Grease and line a deep 8 inch (20cm) cake tin with greased greaseproof paper.

Put the margarine, sugar, flour, eggs and baking powder in a large bowl and beat well for about 2 minutes until thoroughly mixed. Divide the mixture in half. To one half add the cocoa and milk and to the other half add the orange rind and juice. Mix each well.

Put tablespoonfuls of the chocolate and orange mixtures alternately into the prepared tin. Cut through the mixture several times with a knife to slightly blend the mixtures together. Bake in the oven for about 50 minutes until well risen and the cake springs back when lightly pressed with a finger. Cool in the tin for about 5 minutes and then turn out, remove paper and finish cooling on a wire rack.

Hedgehog Cake

Good to serve as a child's birthday cake. A cake baked in a pudding basin lends itself well to form the base of an animal's body. From hedgehogs you can always progress to cats and rabbits!

1oz (25g) cocoa
2 tablespoons hot water
6oz (175g) soft margarine
6oz (175g) caster sugar
3 eggs, lightly beaten
5oz (150g) self-raising flour
1 teaspoon baking powder

FOR THE ICING AND DECORATION
4oz (100g) butter, softened
8oz (225g) icing sugar,sieved
2oz (50g) drinking chocolate
1 large packet chocolate buttons
1 glacé cherry
2 seedless raisins

Heat the oven to 350°F/180°C/Gas Mark 4. Lightly grease a 2 pint (1·2 litre) ovenproof pudding basin.

For the cake, measure the cocoa and hot water into a large bowl and mix well to blend. Add the remaining ingredients and beat well for 2 minutes, then turn into the prepared basin. Level the top and bake in the oven for about 1 hour until the top springs back when lightly pressed with a finger. Leave in the basin to cool for about 5 minutes, then turn out and finish cooling on a wire rack.

For the icing, put the butter, sugar and drinking chocolate into a bowl and mix well until thoroughly blended.

To assemble the hedgehog, spread the flat side of the cake with butter icing, then cut in half down the middle and sandwich the two iced sides together to form the body. Stand on a serving dish. Spread the remaining icing over the whole of the cake, forming one end into a 'snout' with a little extra icing. Arrange the chocolate buttons over three-quarters of the cake to form the spines. Mark the face with a fork and use the cherry for the nose and the raisins for the eyes.

Chocolate Cup Cakes

MAKES ABOUT 35

A great favourite for tea. Ice the cakes while they are still in the patty tins.

1 rounded tablespoon cocoa, sieved
2 tablespoons hot water
4oz (100g) soft margarine
1 level teaspoon baking powder
6oz (175g) self-raising flour
6oz (175g) caster sugar
2 eggs
4 tablespoons milk

FOR THE ICING
4oz (100g) plain chocolate, broken into small pieces
4 tablespoons water
1oz (25g) butter
6oz (175g) icing sugar, sieved

Heat the oven to 350°F/180°C/Gas Mark 4. Use about 35 paper cases to line patty tins.

Blend the cocoa with the water in a large mixing bowl then add the remaining ingredients. Beat well for about 2 minutes until thoroughly mixed. Divide the cake mixture between the paper cases then bake in the oven for about 15 minutes until cakes spring back when lightly pressed with the finger. Allow to cool in the tins.

For the icing, put the plain chocolate, water and butter in a bowl and allow to melt gently over a pan of simmering water. Remove from heat and beat in icing sugar until smooth. Allow to cool then pour a layer on top of each of the cakes. Allow the icing to set before lifting them out of the tins.

Chocolate Brownies

MAKES 16 SQUARES

Real American, very sweet, crumbly brownies. Always popular.

2 eggs
8oz (225g) caster sugar
3 tablespoons cocoa, sieved
3oz (75g) soft margarine
2oz (50g) self-raising flour
4oz (100g) sultanas
4oz (100g) chopped walnuts

FOR THE ICING
1½oz (40g) butter
1oz (25g) cocoa, sieved
2 tablespoons milk
4oz (100g) icing sugar, sieved

Heat the oven to 350°F/180°C/Gas Mark 4.

Put all the ingredients for the brownies in a bowl and beat well until thoroughly mixed. Turn into a well greased 9 inch (22·5cm) square tin, and smooth the top. Bake in the oven for about 35 minutes until the mixture has shrunk from the sides of the tin and is firm to the touch. Leave to cool.

For the icing, melt the butter in a pan, then stir in the cocoa and cook gently for a minute. Remove from the heat, stir in the milk and icing sugar and beat well until smooth. Cool, stirring occasionally, until thick enough to spread over the brownie. Leave to set, then mark brownie into 16 squares.

Walnut Meringue Biscuits

MAKES ABOUT 30 BISCUITS

These are a delicious, rich, crunchy biscuit. As walnuts are expensive to buy they can be omitted from the cream leaving it plain.

5 egg whites
7oz (200g) caster sugar
4oz (100g) walnuts, finely chopped
2 rounded tablespoons flour

FOR THE CREAM FILLING
2oz (50g) butter
2oz (50g) caster sugar
2oz (50g) plain chocolate, broken into small pieces
2oz (50g) walnuts, finely chopped

Heat the oven to 350°F/180°C/Gas Mark 4, and line 2 baking sheets with silicone paper.

First make the meringue mixture. Whisk the egg whites until stiff, then gradually add the sugar, a teaspoonful at a time, whisking well after each addition. Gently fold in the walnuts and flour until thoroughly blended. Put the mixture into a piping bag fitted with a ½ inch (1·25cm) plain nozzle. Pipe about 60 small rounds onto the baking sheets. Bake in the oven for about 20 minutes until a crust has formed on top. Lift off trays onto a cooling tray to cool.

Meanwhile prepare the cream filling. Cream butter and sugar together until light. Melt chocolate in a bowl over a pan of gently simmering water then remove from heat. Allow to cool slightly then stir in to the creamed mixture with the walnuts. Leave to cool and thicken a little, then sandwich the meringue biscuits together with the cream.

Chocolate Caramel Shortbread

MAKES 21 FINGERS

This shortbread takes time to make, but it is well worth the effort.

4oz (100g) soft margarine
2oz (50g) caster sugar 6oz (175g) plain flour

FOR THE CARAMEL

4oz (100g) hard margarine 3oz (75g) caster sugar
2 level tablespoons golden syrup
6·9oz (196g) can condensed milk

FOR THE TOPPING

4oz (100g) plain chocolate, broken into small pieces

Heat the oven to 350°F/180°C/Gas Mark 4. Grease a Swiss roll tin, 7 × 11 inches (17·5 × 27·5cm).

Put the margarine, sugar and flour in a bowl and knead together to form a firm dough. Press into the tin with the palms of your hands. Prick with a fork then bake for about 25 minutes until golden brown.

While the shortbread is baking, put the caramel ingredients in a pan, heat gently until melted, then boil the mixture for about 8 minutes until a caramel colour. Stir continuously, preferably with a flat based wooden spoon which can get into the sides of the pan and prevent the mixture from catching. Leave to cool slightly. When the shortbread is cooked and has cooled for about 5 minutes, pour caramel over it and leave on one side.

Melt the chocolate in a bowl over a pan of gently simmering water. Remove from heat and pour in a steady stream over the caramel and with a fork lightly make a swirling pattern. Leave for several hours then divide into 21 slices.

Chocolate Crunch Cake

A very versatile recipe, which will be popular with all the family. It can be served decorated with whipped cream as a cake, or as a pudding with pouring cream. It can also be cut in wedges for the childrens' packed lunch boxes.

For special occasions add 2 tablespoons brandy to the chocolate after melting.

8oz (225g) digestive or broken biscuits
2oz (50g) walnuts, lightly chopped
2oz (50g) glacé cherries, chopped
4oz (100g) marshmallows, snipped with wet scissors
10oz (275g) plain chocolate, broken into small pieces
4oz (100g) butter

Roughly break up the digestive biscuits. Put in a large bowl with walnuts, cherries and marshmallows.

Put 9oz (250g) of the chocolate with the butter in a bowl over a pan of simmering water. Leave until melted. When melted, stir until smooth and glossy, then pour over biscuit and nut mixture. Mix well until all the pieces are coated. Turn into a loose-bottomed plain or fluted 9 inch (22·5cm) flan tin. Smooth over the top with a fork whilst still warm, and grate remaining 1oz (25g) chocolate over the surface. Leave until cold and set.

Remove the cake from the tin by quickly dipping the base into very hot water for a couple of seconds. Turn cake out onto a plate.

Chocolate Tiffin

MAKES 16 PIECES

Chocolate tiffin is good to include in a packed lunch or to take on a picnic. I often make a tray when the children bring back friends for tea: they all adore it. The children can also make it themselves during the school holidays when they are in need of something to do!

4oz (100g) hard margarine
3 level tablespoons golden syrup
1oz (25g) drinking chocolate
2oz (50g) marshmallows, snipped in small pieces
8oz (225g) digestive biscuits, crushed
6oz (175g) plain chocolate, broken into small pieces

Line a shallow 7 × 11 inch (17·5 × 27·5cm) tin with foil.

Put the margarine, syrup and drinking chocolate in a pan and heat until the margarine has melted. Remove from the heat and cool slightly, then stir in the marshmallows and biscuits. Mix thoroughly and then turn into the tin, press down firmly and chill until firm.

Melt the chocolate in a bowl over a pan of simmering water, then spread evenly over the biscuit base and leave until set. Peel off the foil, then divide tiffin into 16 pieces.

Chocolate Crunchies

MAKES ABOUT 15

The children love making these, and they're always a favourite at teatime or at a birthday-party tea. I make these with whatever ingredients I happen to have in the store cupboard: if I haven't enough almonds or sultanas then I use walnuts and raisins instead. It is often a good idea to wait until the biscuit tin is running low and then use up any broken biscuits which have worked their way to the bottom of the tin.

6oz (175g) milk chocolate, broken into pieces
5oz (150g) hard margarine
1 egg
1oz (25g) caster sugar
6oz (175g) digestive biscuits
1oz (25g) almonds, chopped
2oz (50g) sultanas
1oz (25g) glacé cherries, quartered

Melt the chocolate with the margarine in a bowl over a pan of simmering water. Beat egg and sugar together and gradually add the cooled, melted chocolate mixture.

Break up biscuits until quite small, but not crumbled, and stir in along with the almonds, sultanas and cherries. Spoon into 15 paper cake cases, and chill overnight.

Peanut Butter Bars

MAKES 28 BARS

I have to confess I am not a peanut butter fan. However, the children just loved these bars and couldn't wait for them to be made again. They are also good made with half granulated sugar and half demerara sugar.

Not everyone likes the flavour of chocolate cake covering, so if preferred use melted chocolate or a chocolate fudge icing instead – like that for Chocolate Cup Cakes (see page 56).

8oz (225g) crunchy peanut butter
8oz (225g) granulated sugar
1 egg
4oz (100g) chocolate cake covering, broken into small pieces

Heat the oven to 325°F/160°C/Gas Mark 3.

Beat peanut butter, sugar and egg together in a bowl until well mixed. Press this mixture into an 11 × 7 inch (27·5 × 17·5cm) tin and level out with a palette knife or the back of a spoon.

Bake in the oven for about 20 minutes until a pale golden brown. Allow to cool.

Put chocolate in a bowl over a pan of simmering water and leave until melted. Spread this over the cooled biscuit base, and decorate by swirling with a fork in a zig-zag pattern. Allow to harden, then divide into 28 bars.

Chocolate and Cherry Cookies

MAKES ABOUT 30

A delicious light biscuit with a couple of excellent variations.

3oz (75g) soft margarine
3oz (75g) light muscovado sugar
3oz (75g) demerara sugar
1 egg, beaten
6oz (175g) self-raising flour
2oz (50g) glacé cherries, chopped
2oz (50g) plain chocolate dots

Heat the oven to 350°F/180°C/Gas Mark 4.

Put all the ingredients together in a bowl and mix well until thoroughly blended. Take teaspoonfuls of the mixture, roll into balls, then arrange on 2 or 3 lightly greased baking trays, leaving room for them to spread.

Bake in the oven for about 20 minutes until a pale golden brown colour. Leave to cool on the trays for about 3 minutes then lift off with a palette knife onto a wire rack to finish cooling.

Chocolate and Walnut Cookies
Omit the glacé cherries and add 2oz (50g) chopped walnuts to the mixture instead.

Wholemeal Chocolate and Cherry Cookies
Omit 4oz (100g) of the self-raising flour and add 4oz (100g) wholemeal flour and 1 level teaspoon baking powder to the mixture.

Mocha Cookies

MAKES ABOUT 40

These are a cross between a rock cake and a biscuit. Children simply adore them, and you'll undoubtedly be asked to make them again!

8oz (225g) self-raising flour
2oz (50g) plain flour
4oz (100g) butter
3oz (75g) caster sugar
3oz (75g) chocolate dots
1 egg, beaten
2 tablespoons coffee essence
2 tablespoons milk

Heat the oven to 375°F/190°C/Gas Mark 5, and lightly grease 2 or 3 baking trays.

Put the flours in a bowl and rub in the butter until the mixture resembles fine breadcrumbs. Stir in the sugar and chocolate dots, then mix to a firm dough with the egg, coffee essence and milk. Take teaspoonfuls of the mixture and pile in small rounds on the baking trays.

Bake in the oven for about 20 minutes until a golden brown colour. Leave on the trays to cool slightly then lift off with a palette knife and finish cooling on a wire rack.

Speckled Chocolate Biscuits

MAKES ABOUT 30

A crisp, mildly chocolate flavoured biscuit, which will keep well in an airtight tin.

8oz (225g) plain flour
1 level teaspoon baking powder
4oz (100g) soft margarine
6oz (175g) caster sugar
2oz (50g) plain chocolate, coarsely grated
1 egg, beaten
a few teaspoons of milk, if necessary

Put the flour in a bowl with the baking powder, then rub in the margarine until the mixture resembles fine breadcrumbs. Add sugar and chocolate then bind together with the egg and sufficient milk to form a firm dough. Knead until smooth then roll into a long sausage shape about 2 inches (5cm) wide. Wrap in clingfilm and chill in the refrigerator for about 3 hours until firm.

Heat the oven to 375°F/190°C/Gas Mark 5.

Remove clingfilm and cut sausage into about 30 slices. Arrange on lightly greased baking trays, leaving room for them to spread, then cook in the oven for about 20 minutes until a pale golden brown. Leave to cool on the trays for a few moments then lift off with a palette knife onto a wire rack to finish cooling. Store in an airtight container.

Country Nut Bars

MAKES 16 BARS

These are quite substantial biscuits, a treat to give the children for their school break or in a packed lunch.

4oz (100g) soft margarine
6oz (175g) light muscovado sugar
1 egg, beaten
8oz (225g) self-raising flour
3oz (75g) plain chocolate, coarsely grated
3oz (75g) chopped mixed nuts

Heat the oven to 375°F/190°C/Gas Mark 5, and lightly grease a 7 × 11 inch (17·5 × 27·5cm) Swiss roll tin.

Put all the ingredients into a large bowl and mix well until thoroughly blended. It may be easiest to do this with your hands.

Turn mixture into the prepared tin and press down firmly so that the top is level. Bake in the oven for about 20 minutes until golden brown.

Cool slightly in the tin then cut into 16 bars. Lift out with a palette knife and finish cooling on a wire rack.

Chocolate Viennese Biscuits

MAKES ABOUT 30 BISCUITS

I often get the children to help with making these – they love to dip the biscuits in the chocolate.

8oz (225g) soft margarine
2oz (50g) icing sugar
8oz (225g) plain flour
4oz (100g) plain chocolate, melted

Heat the oven to 325°F/160°C/Gas Mark 3. Lightly grease 2 baking sheets.

Measure the margarine, sugar and flour into a bowl and rub in the margarine until the mixture resembles fine breadcrumbs. Knead together with your hand until it forms a smooth soft mixture. Place the mixture in a piping bag fitted with a large star nozzle and pipe out into 2 inch (5cm) lengths.

Bake the biscuits in the oven for about 20 minutes until tinged a pale golden brown at the edges. Remove from the oven, leave to harden for a minute then lift carefully off with a palette knife and leave to cool on a wire rack.

When quite cold, dip the ends of the biscuits in the melted chocolate and leave to set on baking parchment.

Florentines

MAKES ABOUT 12

These are tricky to make so be sure to allow yourself plenty of time. They will spread in the oven during cooking, so space them well apart on the baking trays. They are easily pushed into shape with a palette knife when they come out of the oven: this is best done as soon as they are cooked as they become more difficult to handle as they cool.

2oz (50g) butter
2oz (50g) caster sugar
2oz (50g) mixed walnuts and blanched almonds, finely chopped
1oz (25g) candied peel, chopped
3 glacé cherries, chopped
1oz (25g) sultanas, chopped
1 tablespoon single cream
3oz (75g) plain chocolate, broken into small pieces

Heat the oven to 350°F/180°C/Gas Mark 4.

Melt the butter in a small pan, add the sugar and boil for 1 minute. Stir in the mixed chopped nuts, peel, cherries and sultanas with the cream, and mix well until evenly coated. Put teaspoonfuls of the mixture on 2–3 well greased baking trays, leaving plenty of room for them to spread. Cook in the oven for about 10 minutes until golden brown. Take out of oven and push into rounds with a palette knife. Allow to cool slightly then lift onto a wire rack to finish cooling.

Melt the chocolate gently in a bowl over a pan of simmering water, remove from the heat and spread over the backs of the florentines with a knife. Allow to set slightly then make wavy zig-zag patterns in the chocolate with a fork. Leave to set.

SPECIAL CAKES

Sunday Best Chocolate Cake

A really rich chocolate flavoured cake. It keeps well in an airtight tin.

6½oz (190g) self-raising flour
1 teaspoon baking powder
5oz (150g) caster sugar
2 eggs
5oz (150g) hard margarine, melted and cooled
¼ pt (150ml) milk
2 tablespoons golden syrup
2 rounded tablespoons cocoa, sieved
about 2 tablespoons apricot jam
chocolate flake or curls, to decorate

FOR THE ICING AND FILLING
6oz (175g) margarine
4 rounded tablespoons cocoa, sieved
2 rounded tablespoons golden syrup

Heat the oven to 325°F/160°C/Gas Mark 3. Grease and line 2 × 8 inch (20cm) sandwich tins with greased greaseproof paper.

Beat all the ingredients for the cake – except for the apricot jam and chocolate flake – together in a bowl until smooth. Divide between the tins and bake in the oven for about 40 minutes or until cake springs back when pressed and come away from the sides of the tins. Remove from oven, and turn out onto a wire rack. Cool and then remove the papers. Spread one sponge with apricot jam.

For the icing and filling, cream all the ingredients together in a saucepan over a low heat. Cool. When just beginning to thicken, spread half the mixture on the sponge on top of the jam. Cover with the other sponge and spread the rest of the icing on top of the cake. Decorate with chocolate flake or curls.

Rich Real Chocolate Cakes

MAKES 2 CAKES

This mixture makes 2 shallow cakes which are very moist and special – so to be served in small slices. They freeze well for up to 2 months.

10oz (275g) plain chocolate, broken into small pieces
8oz (225g) unsalted butter
grated rind and juice of 1 small orange   5 eggs
8oz (225g) caster sugar, warmed
4oz (100g) McDougalls fine cake flour

CHOCOLATE ICING
5oz (150g) unsalted butter
6oz (175g) plain chocolate, broken into small pieces
2 tablespoons Cointreau or other orange liqueur
1 tablespoon orange juice

Heat the oven to 350°F/180°C/Gas Mark 4. Grease 2 × 8 inch (20cm) sandwich tins and line with greased greaseproof paper.

For the cakes, put the chocolate, butter, orange rind and juice in a bowl and stand over a pan of simmering water until melted. Beat well with a wooden spoon until smooth, then stand on one side.

Break the eggs into a large bowl, add sugar, then whisk for about 3 minutes until light and foamy. Gently stir in the chocolate mixture and then the flour. Divide mixture between the tins and bake in the oven for about 50 minutes. The cakes will be well risen and will have a brittle crunchy top. Cool in the tin for about 5 minutes then turn cakes out, remove paper, and finish cooling on a wire rack.

For the icing, put the butter and chocolate in a small bowl and stand over a pan of simmering water until melted. Remove from heat, stir in Cointreau and orange juice, then beat until smooth. Allow to cool until a spreading consistency, then spread icing over the two sponges.

Devil's Food Cake

A very sweet cake, so serve cut into fairly small wedges.

3½oz (90g) plain flour
1 level teaspoon baking powder
1 tablespoon cocoa, sieved
2½oz (65g) caster sugar
1 tablespoon golden syrup
1 egg, beaten
6 tablespoons sunflower oil
6 tablespoons milk

FOR THE FROSTING
12oz (350g) caster sugar
2 egg whites
4 tablespoons water
½ teaspoon cream of tartar
a few drops vanilla essence

Heat the oven to 325°F/160°C/Gas Mark 3. Grease and line with greased greaseproof paper 2 × 7 inch (17·5cm) sandwich tins.

Put all the cake ingredients in a bowl and beat well to form a smooth batter. Divide between the tins and bake in the oven for about 35 minutes until the tops spring back when lightly pressed with a finger. Turn out and leave to cool on a wire rack.

For the frosting, measure all the ingredients into a bowl standing over simmering water. Stir until the sugar has dissolved then whisk with an electric whisk until mixture stands in peaks. Sandwich the cakes together with some of the icing then cover the top and sides with the remainder.

Swiss Chocolate Cake

This cake sinks when you take it out of the oven so expect it to!

6 large eggs, separated
5oz (150g) caster sugar, warmed
2oz (50g) cocoa, sieved
1½oz (40g) cooking chocolate
½ pt (300ml) whipping cream, whipped

Heat the oven to 350°F/180°C/Gas Mark 4. Grease and line with greased greaseproof paper 2 × 8 inch (20cm) sandwich tins.

Put the egg whites in a large bowl and the yolks in a smaller bowl. Add caster sugar and cocoa to the yolks, and whisk until thick. Whisk whites with an electric or rotary whisk until mixture forms stiff peaks. Mix a little of the whisked whites with the yolks, then add the yolk mixture to the egg whites and fold with a metal spoon until thoroughly blended.

Gently turn into the tins and bake in the oven for about 25 minutes until just beginning to shrink back from the sides of the tins. Remove and leave to cool in the tins for 5 minutes. Turn out on to wire racks and remove paper.

While they are cooling make the chocolate curls or carque with the chocolate (see page 13).

Sandwich the cooled cakes together with half the cream then spread the remainder on top. Decorate with chocolate caraque. Keep cake cool until served.

Sachertorte

The cake has a close texture and is rich, dark and special. Serve with whipped cream.

3½oz (90g) butter 5oz (150g) caster sugar
5 eggs, separated
4oz (100g) plain chocolate, broken into small pieces
1 tablespoon rum
3oz (75g) hazelnuts, finely chopped
3oz (75g) fresh brown breadcrumbs
10oz (275g) apricot jam

FOR THE ICING
2oz (50g) plain chocolate, broken into small pieces
2 tablespoons water ½oz (15g) butter
about 3oz (75g) icing sugar, sieved

Heat the oven to 400°F/200°C/Gas Mark 6. Grease and line with greased greaseproof paper a 9 inch (22·5cm) deep cake tin.

For the cake, put butter and sugar in a bowl and beat well until light. Gradually beat in egg yolks. Put chocolate and rum in a bowl over a pan of simmering water and melt. Allow to cool slightly, then fold into creamed mixture with nuts and breadcrumbs. Whisk egg whites in a bowl until they form stiff peaks then fold them into chocolate mixture.

Turn into prepared tin and bake in the oven for 35 minutes until well risen and firm to the touch. Cool in tin for about 15 minutes then turn out onto a wire rack. Remove the paper. When cool, divide into 3 layers and sandwich together generously with the jam.

For the icing, put chocolate, water and butter in a bowl and stand over simmering water until melted. Beat until smooth, then stir in enough icing sugar to give a coating consistency. Spread evenly over cake.

Black Forest Gâteau

This is a large cake which should serve at least 12 people, and is very special indeed.

4 eggs
4oz (100g) caster sugar, warmed
1½oz (40g) ground almonds
1oz (25g) cocoa, sieved
2½oz (65g) self-raising flour 1oz (25g) butter, melted

FOR THE FILLING AND ICING
3 tablespoons Kirsch
14oz (397g) can black cherry pie filling
1 pt (600ml) whipping cream, whipped
chocolate caraque (see page 13), to decorate

Heat the oven to 400°F/200°C/Gas Mark 6. Line a deep 9 inch (22·5cm) cake tin with greased greaseproof paper.

For the sponge, whisk the eggs in a bowl with an electric whisk for a minute, then add sugar and continue whisking for about 5 minutes until the mixture forms a thick foam. Gently stir in almonds, cocoa and flour, then add melted butter. Turn mixture into prepared tin. Reduce oven to 375°F/190°C/Gas Mark 5 and bake sponge for about 30 minutes until well risen and it springs back when lightly pressed. Allow to cool in tin for 5 minutes then turn out on to a wire rack. Remove paper.

Divide cake into 3 layers. Soak the first layer with half the Kirsch then spread with half the cherry filling and a layer of whipped cream. Cover with second layer of sponge and repeat with Kirsch, cherry filling and cream. Cover with third layer of sponge, and spread remaining cream around the sides and on top. Decorate with chocolate caraque. Keep cool until served.

SWEETS, CONFECTIONS AND SAUCES

Chocolate and Date Praline Pieces

MAKES ABOUT 30 PIECES

These small chocolate and date squares are good to eat with a cup of coffee.

4oz (100g) margarine
2oz (50g) light muscovado sugar
3oz (75g) chopped dates
1oz (25g) cocoa, sieved
8oz (225g) digestive biscuits, made into crumbs
6oz (175g) plain chocolate, broken into small pieces

Melt margarine in a saucepan with the sugar, then add the dates. Mix this thoroughly with a wooden spoon until the margarine is completely incorporated into a smooth mixture. Add cocoa, then stir in the crushed biscuits and combine thoroughly.

Press mixture out into a 9 × 11 inch (22·5 × 27·5cm) Swiss roll tin with a palette knife or the back of a metal spoon to give a smooth surface. Chill until firm.

Melt chocolate in a basin over a pan of simmering water. When melted spread evenly over biscuit base. Decorate by swirling lines along the top with a fork. Leave to set and mark into about 30 pieces.

Honey, Fruit and Nut Clusters

MAKES ABOUT 15

These fruit and nut clusters make sticky rich sweets to go with coffee.

2oz (50g) plain chocolate, broken into small pieces
2oz (50g) thick honey
3oz (75g) walnuts, roughly chopped
2oz (50g) glacé cherries, roughly chopped
1oz (25g) raisins

Melt chocolate and honey together in a bowl over a pan of simmering water. Once melted remove from heat and stir in the walnuts, cherries and raisins.

Chill the mixture in the refrigerator until it is firm enough to mould into clusters. (Use spoon and fingers.) Put each sweet in a petits-fours case to serve.

Chocolate Brandy Truffles

MAKES ABOUT 50

If you have any plain sponge cake that has been in the cake tin for too long, then this is a good way of using it up. The truffles are ideal to give as presents for birthdays or Christmas: pack them in small polythene bags and tie with a pretty ribbon, or in clean margarine tubs, covered with clingfilm and decorate with a bow.

6oz (175g) plain chocolate, broken into small pieces
2oz (50g) butter
3 level tablespoons golden syrup
8 tablespoons brandy
4oz (100g) ground almonds
12oz (350g) Madeira cake, crumbled
chocolate vermicelli

Put the chocolate, butter and syrup in a bowl and stand over a pan of simmering water until melted. Remove from the heat and stir in the brandy, almonds and cake crumbs. Mix well, then chill in the refrigerator until the mixture is firm and manageable.

Spread the vermicelli on a plate. Take a teaspoonful of the mixture, shape it into a ball and roll and coat evenly in the vermicelli. Put each in a petits-fours case – you'll need about 50 – and chill in the refrigerator until really firm.

Chocolate Brazils

Rather than using all plain chocolate you could coat half the nuts in milk chocolate as a contrast to the plain. They make a lovely present if put in paper sweet cases and packed in a pretty box in a single layer.

about 3oz (75g) plain chocolate, broken into small pieces
4oz (100g) whole Brazil nuts

Melt the chocolate in a bowl over a pan of simmering water. Remove from the heat.

Spear a nut with a long fine skewer and then dip into the melted chocolate, turning so that the nut is completely coated. Knock gently on the side of the bowl so that any surplus chocolate drips off.

Gently ease the nut from the skewer onto a piece of waxed paper and leave in a cool place to set. Repeat with the remaining nuts and chocolate.

Fresh Fruit Chocolates

These are good to serve with coffee after a meal and also make very attractive decorations on fresh cream cakes.

fresh strawberries
firm pears, peeled, cored and sliced
under-ripe bananas, sliced
seedless grapes
melted plain chocolate

Choose any variety of fruits, I find those suggested above most acceptable. Prepare each fruit accordingly: the strawberries should be left with their stalks on; pears need peeling, coring and slicing; peel and slice the bananas fairly thickly; just wash and dry the grapes.

To coat the fruits with chocolate, stab the fruit with a cocktail stick and dip into the melted chocolate. Allow any excess to drip back, then stand the fruits on silicone paper to set. Serve the fruits still on their cocktail sticks as this saves sticky fingers. I like to partly cover the fruits with chocolate so that you can still see the colour of the fruit. Best eaten soon after they are made.

Colettes

MAKES ABOUT 24

Very special chocolates with which to end a meal. Keep in the refrigerator for up to 1 week.

6oz (175g) plain chocolate, broken into small pieces
about 24 hazelnuts, to decorate

FOR THE FILLING
¼ pt (150ml) double cream
10oz (275g) plain chocolate, broken into small pieces
2 tablespoons brandy or rum
2oz (50g) butter

First prepare the chocolate cases. Have ready about 24 petits-fours wax or silicone treated paper cases. Put the 6oz (175g) chocolate in a bowl over a pan of simmering water and allow to melt. Remove from heat then, using the handle of a teaspoon, spread the chocolate round the base and sides of each petits-fours case to give a smooth coating. Chill in the refrigrator to set.

Now prepare the filling. Put the cream in a bowl and stand over a pan of simmering water. When cream has almost reached boiling point, add the chocolate and stir until it has all melted. Add the brandy or rum and butter, and continue to stir until mixture forms a thick smooth cream. Remove from heat and leave to cool.

Put filling in a piping bag fitted with a large star nozzle and pipe a rosette of filling in each chocolate case. Top with a hazelnut. Keep in the refrigerator until required.

Simple Chocolate Peppermint Creams

MAKES ABOUT 20

These are an ideal way of using up royal icing after cake decorating (although they're delicious to make anyway!): just add some extra icing sugar until the icing is thick and pliable, and work in a few drops of peppermint essence. Then continue as suggested in the recipe.

8oz (225g) icing sugar
1 egg white, lightly beaten
a few drops peppermint essence
4oz (100g) plain chocolate, melted

Sift the icing sugar into a bowl and then stir in sufficient egg white to make a paste. Add a few drops of peppermint essence and knead well. The mixture should be thick and pliable.

Sieve a little extra sugar onto a piece of silicone paper, place the peppermint paste on the paper, cover with another piece of paper, and roll out to ¼ inch (6mm) thickness. Remove top sheet of paper and cut into 1 inch (2·5cm) diameter rounds.

Leave in a dry place overnight to dry out thoroughly then dip in melted chocolate and leave to set on a sheet of silicone paper.

Easter Eggs

Plastic egg moulds are not expensive to buy and can be used time and time again. It is fun to make your own eggs to give as presents at Easter and they are appreciated so much more than the packaged ones you can buy in shops.

melted chocolate
plastic egg moulds

Polish the moulds with a cloth so they are spotlessly clean. Pour a little chocolate into the bottom of the mould and spread out thinly and evenly. Stand in the refrigerator to set. Repeat this with four more layers of chocolate, allowing each layer to set before adding the next.

To unmould the egg, stand the moulds in the freezer for about 5 minutes, when the chocolate will shrink away slightly from the sides. Tip the mould upside down and tap gently on the bottom to release the egg. Trim the rough edges carefully with a very sharp knife. Now is the time to fill one half with a few Smarties or wrapped sweets, if you want to. Join two halves together: spread a little melted chocolate around the edges and sandwich two halves together. Allow to set, then tie a ribbon around the egg to hide the join. The eggs are very fragile so do take great care when handling them.

If liked, you can write the recipient's name on the top of the egg with a little royal icing. Alternately, decorate the top of the egg with a few cut-out chocolate shapes, secured onto the egg with a little melted chocolate.

Fabulous Children's Fudge

MAKES 18 PIECES

A quick and easy chocolate fudge. It's ideal for the children to make themselves as there is no boiling for hours, unlike most fudge recipes. If a less sweet soft fudge is preferred use plain chocolate.

¼ pt (150ml) condensed milk (a small tin)
8 oz (225g) milk chocolate, broken into small pieces
1 teaspoon vanilla essence
2 oz (50g) chopped nuts, if liked

Put the condensed milk and chocolate into a bowl over a pan of simmering water. Stir until the chocolate has melted and the mixture is smooth and thick. Remove from heat and blend in vanilla essence. Stir in the nuts at this stage if used.

Pour into a greased 8 × 4 inch (20 × 10cm) loaf tin, and chill until firm. Mark into 18 squares.

Mocha and Walnut Fudge
Omit the vanilla essence and stir in 2 tablespoons coffee essence and 2oz (50g) roughly chopped walnuts (instead of the chopped nuts).

Cherry and Chocolate Fudge
Stir 2oz (50g) chopped glacé cherries into the basic mixture just before pouring into the tin.

Chocolate Fudge

MAKES ABOUT 36 SQUARES

Fudge makes a special present for birthdays or Christmas. It is always nice to receive things that are home-made.

1oz (25g) cocoa
¼ pt (150ml) evaporated milk
¼ pt (150ml) water
3oz (75g) butter
1lb (450g) granulated sugar

Put the cocoa in a pan and blend to a smooth paste with the evaporated milk. Add the remaining ingredients and heat through slowly, without boiling, until the butter has melted and the sugar dissolved.

Increase heat and bring to the boil, stirring constantly so that the fudge does not stick. If you have a sugar thermometer then allow the fudge to reach 237°F/114°C, otherwise drop a small amount of the fudge into a cup of cold water. When the fudge forms a soft ball in the water then it is ready.

Cool slightly then beat until the mixture starts to thicken and crystallise on the spoon. Pour into a buttered 7 inch (17·5cm) square tin and leave to set. Make into 36 squares.

Swiss Hot Chocolate

SERVES 2

Lovely and warming on a cold winter's night, the addition of a dollop of whipped cream makes this Swiss Hot Chocolate a real treat.

1 pt (600ml) milk
6 heaped teaspoonfuls drinking chocolate
about ⅛ pt (75ml) whipping cream, whipped

Bring the milk up to boiling point in a saucepan, remove from the heat, and then sprinkle on the drinking chocolate and whisk in with a balloon whisk.

Pour chocolate into 2 mugs then spoon a blob of cream on top of each just before serving.

Iced Chocolate Drink

SERVES 6

A lovely refreshing drink on a hot summer's day. A basic chocolate syrup is added to chilled milk.

8oz (225g) caster sugar
½ pt (300ml) water
2oz (50g) cocoa, sieved
1 teaspoon instant coffee powder
2 pts (1·2 litres) cold milk

Dissolve the sugar in the water in a pan over a gentle heat. When sugar has completely dissolved, increase heat and boil without stirring for about 8 minutes until a thin syrup is formed. Allow to cool slightly then blend into the cocoa and coffee powder in a bowl. Return to the pan and bring to the boil, stirring until thickened. Simmer for about 3 minutes to cook the cocoa. Remove from the heat and chill well.

To serve, dilute the chocolate syrup with cold milk and serve in chilled glasses.

Chocolate Sauce

SERVES 6

Store this in the refrigerator until required, then warm through before serving with ice cream or profiteroles.

12oz (350g) light muscovado sugar
4 level tablespoons cocoa, sieved
4oz (100g) butter
4 tablespoons golden syrup
¼ pt (150ml) milk

Gently heat all ingredients in a pan until butter has melted and the sugar has dissolved. Boil rapidly for about 1 minute until syrupy. Cool, then store until required.

Mars Bar Sauce

SERVES 6

This is an instant chocolate sauce, so easy to make and good to serve over ice creams and puddings. I try not to think about the calories.

2 Mars bars

Roughly chop the Mars bars and place in a saucepan. Heat gently over a low heat until melted, stirring occasionally to prevent sticking. Serve straight from the pan over ice creams, cakes and creamy puddings.

Chocolate Custard Sauce

MAKES ½ PT (300ML)

This is a useful recipe to have to serve over ice cream and fruits such as pears, or to use in a trifle or on a hot pudding.

2 level tablespoons cocoa, sieved
2 level tablespoons custard powder
3 tablespoons caster sugar
½ pt (300ml) milk

Measure the cocoa, custard powder and sugar into a bowl and blend with a little milk to give a smooth paste.

Heat the remaining milk in a pan until almost boiling then pour onto the paste, mix well and return to the pan. Bring to the boil, stirring until thickened.

Cook for 2 minutes then serve either hot or cold as required.

INDEX